Copyright © 2022 Arthur Ave Publishing

All rights reserved. No part of this publication may be reproduced, distributed, or transmitted in any form or by any means, including photocopying, recording, or other electronic or mechanical methods, without the prior written permission of the publisher, except in the case of brief quotations embodied in critical reviews and certain other noncommercial uses permitted by copyright law. For permission requests, write to the publisher, addressed "Attention: Book Rights and Permission," at the address below.

Published in the United States of America

ISBN 978-1-956741-98-8 (HC)

Arthur Ave Publishing
222 West 6th Street
Suite 400, San Pedro, CA, 90731
www.dannyfalconebooks.com

Order Information and Rights Permission:
Quantity sales. Special discounts might be available on quantity purchases by corporations, associations, and others. For details, contact the publisher at the address above.

For Book Rights Adaptation and other Rights Permission. Call us at toll-free 1-888-945-8513 or send us an email at admin@stellarliterary.com.

Photographs by Dylan Johnson
Designed by Kenna Gabor

Editing by Malory Wood of The Missing Ink Company
Recipes by Danny Falcone & Gerard Gravano
Everything tasted by Sammy 😊 😊 😊

This is a special book. Nothing like it has ever been done before, and most likely will never be done again. It is truly one of a kind. Sammy The Bull Gravano and Danny Falcone are two old mob soldiers both retired from the life. They are old friends and have 40+ years of collective restaurant experience between them. Danny jokes by saying, "Thirty years ago, if the two of us collaborated on a project, that meant someone was gonna get hurt and the F.B.I. would have been working overtime. Today, with the collaboration of this cookbook, no one is in trouble and the only thing the F.B.I. would want now is to taste these delicious Italian dishes."

With each recipe, Sammy adds a personal note on how the dish relates to the mafia. Some of the most famous mob hits have been in restaurants, and the focus is on the dish the mobster was eating at the time of the hit along with some new and exciting recipes to add to your routine.

Italian food is arguably the best cuisine in the world. With Sammy's Sicilian roots and Danny's Napolitano heritage, they bring the best of Italy to life in this cookbook—because Sicily and Napoli without a doubt have some of the best Italian dishes. Italian restaurants worldwide serve their high-class meals for top dollar yet interestingly enough, most of these dishes started out as peasant food to feed the workers. The barons would give unused scraps of meat to the cooks who would feed dozens of land workers. And the rest is history.

Dive into Sammy and Danny's Storytime Cookbook…and mangia!

Table of Contents

7	Smoked Salmon Sriracha Crackers
9	Sundried Tomato Pesto Salad
11	Baccala Salad
13	Escarole And Bean Soup
15	Meatballs
17	Linguine Clam Sauce
19	Fettuccine in Cream Sauce
21	Tortellini In Cream Sauce
23	Chicken Pepperoni
25	Mussels Fra Diavolo
27	Sicilian Rigatoni
29	Lemon Baked Branzino
31	Eggplant Parmesan
33	Veal Chops La Toro
35	Roasted Chicken Sausage
37	Steak Pizziola
39	Paprika Chicken With Chichi Beans
41	Cannoli
43	Zeppoles

SMOKED SALMON SRIRACHA CRACKERS

INGREDIENTS
1 - 4 oz pack smoked salmon
1 - 8 oz package cream cheese
1 - oz Sriracha sauce (adjust to how you like the heat)
1 - box of your favorite crackers
1 - small jar of capers

INSTRUCTIONS
In a bowl mix the cream cheese and Sriracha sauce. Scoop a half teaspoon or so onto each cracker. Cut the salmon into strips (about pinky size). Wrap the salmon on top of the cracker making a teepee look. Top each one off with a caper and enjoy…

Me and the boys love these little hors d'oeuvres when we're playing cards or watching a game. I first had them at someone's wedding and we've been eating them ever since. Simply delicious!

SUNDRIED TOMATO PESTO PASTA SALAD

INGREDIENTS
- 1 cup sundried tomatoes
- 6 basil leaves
- 1/3 cup parmesan cheese
- ¼ cup of pine nuts
- ¼ cup virgin olive oil (add more if needed)
- 4 garlic cloves
- ¼ TSP Koser salt
- ¼ TSP red pepper flakes
- 1 lemon wedge
- 1 lb. bowtie pasta

INSTRUCTIONS
Pour all ingredients into a food processer with the exception of the lemon (feeding the oil a little at a time).

Cook the pasta al dente and allow it to cool. Once the pasta is cold, add the pesto mix and squeeze the lemon over the top. Mix well and enjoy...

NOTE: You can adjust the dish by adding any ingredient when it is done after you taste it. Also, try cutting fresh mozzarella into small pieces and mixing it into the pasta.

I'm a pasta lover as far back as I can remember, so this sundried tomato pesto on pasta is amazing. Nothing like a good cold pasta dish...

BACCALA SALAD

INGREDIENTS
1 small jar of fire roasted red peppers
1 tiny can of sliced black olives
4 cloves of garlic (chopped in small pieces)
2 stalks of celery sliced thin
2 lbs of baccalaVirgin olive oil, granulated garlic, black pepper, lemon pepper

INSTRUCTIONS
To prepare the baccala, rinse the salt off of it and soak it in cold water for 12 or more hours, (refrigerate during the soaking), changing water 2 to 3 times during the soaking process..
Then boil the baccala to a white flakiness (about 30 minutes).
Cool down the baccala then break it apart by hand in a bowl. Add in the garlic, fire roasted peppers, black olives & celery.
Mix in some virgin olive oil, sprinkle with granulated garlic, lemon pepper and black pepper, enjoy.

Sammy

Each year every crew would have a Christmas party and I would make the rounds with John Gotti and try to show up at each party. The members would all kick up a little something and the Caporegime would give an envelope to The Boss. Baccala is a very traditional Christmas dish for the Italian people. I can't ever remember going to a Christmas party and not having some baccala.

ESCAROLE AND BEAN SOUP

INGREDIENTS

- ½ lb. Ditalini pasta (or any small size pasta, shells, elbow or lumaconi)
- 3 cloves garlic sliced thin
- 1 12 oz can Cannellini beans (white kidney beans)
- 1 head of escarole
- 1 tsp granulated garlic
- 1 pinch salt
- 2 pinches black pepper
- 2 pinches red pepper flakes
- 1 TBSP grated Romano cheese
- 1 tsp chicken base (the paste kind)
- Virgin olive oil
- 6 cans of water from the bean can

INSTRUCTIONS

In a pot, put a very thin layer of virgin olive oil and place on med heat. Add garlic into the pot. Stir garlic and cook for several minutes, throw in the red pepper flakes. As the garlic turns to a golden brown, add the can of beans, liquid and all. (The beans are in a watery paste that we'll want to use!) Use cold water to rinse the can out, scraping the paste at the bottom. Fill the can up with water six times. Next, cut the escarole down the middle, removing the stub, then half it so you have four pieces and half it again leaving it cut into eight pieces. Add it to the beans. When the soup is boiling, add the chicken base and ½ lb. of pasta. Sprinkle in the salt and pepper and cook until the pasta is al dente. That's it! Top it off with the Romano cheese and enjoy…

NOTE: You can also add meat to the soup. Ham, prosciutto or pancetta works best, just add in with the garlic at the beginning of the process.

My goombata Allie Boy loved this traditional Italian dish. He would eat bowls of it and fart for days. One time, we were going on a hit and Allie had eaten escarole & beans. He was farting so badly that we told him he could go on the hit by himself and instead of shooting the guy, he could just go in and fart. That would seal the victim's fate…

MEATBALLS

INGREDIENTS

- 2 lbs. ground beef (chuck)
- 1/3 lbs. ground pork
- 1/3 lbs. ground veal
- 3 eggs
- 1 cup milk
- 1 slice white bread
- 2 cups Italian-seasoned breadcrumbs
- 1/2 cup fresh Italian parsley sprigs, chopped
- 1 cup grated Romano cheese
- 3 TBSP granulated garlic
- 1 TBSP black pepper
- 1 cup olive oil or oil of your choice

INSTRUCTIONS

Pour the milk into a small bowl and add a sprig or two of parsley, a couple of pinches of Romano cheese and a pinch of granulated garlic. Cut the crust off the bread and tear it off into tiny pieces. Add to the milk mixture. In a large bowl, mix the three ground meats together. Be careful to mix the meat well without squeezing it together. Just gently toss the meats until they are well mixed. Add your eggs and all other ingredients except for the breadcrumbs. Pour the milk mixture into the large bowl of meat and mix well—again being careful not to squeeze the meat together too hard. Taste a tiny piece of raw meat to see if you need to add more garlic or grated cheese. Next, roll your meatballs by hand into whatever size you'd like, once again not squeezing them too tight in the process. In a frying pan, put your oil in and turn to medium heat. Fry your meatballs until they are browned and beautiful. Enjoy…

NOTE: The meatballs will be tasty and juicy if they are not compressed together but rather gently shaped.

There have been more than a few Wiseguys over the years nicknamed "Meatballs". The now-deceased Genovese soldier Salvatore "Sammy Meatballs" Aparo, I knew well. Sammy Meatballs was a big man with a big smile and even a bigger set of balls. He was a no-nonsense tough guy all the way.

LINGUINE IN CLAM SAUCE

INGREDIENTS

1 lb. linguine
4 TBSP butter
4 cloves garlic, sliced thinly
½ cup white wine or water
2 pounds littleneck clams
Chopped fresh parsley to garnish (Just sprinkle a little on top, no need to measure)
1 small can of baby clams in water
¼ tsp clam base (paste)
pinch red pepper flakes (optional)

INSTRUCTIONS

Boil pasta until al dente. While pasta is cooking, melt the butter in a large skillet. Add garlic and red pepper flakes, if using, and cook for 1 minute, being careful not to burn the garlic or it will become bitter. Add the white wine or water, bring to a boil and add the clam base and cook to reduce the liquid by half, about 2-3 minutes.

Add the clams, cover with a tight-fitting lid and cook until the clams have opened about 6-8 minutes. Discard any clams that remain unopened. Season with salt and pepper to taste. Add in entire small can of baby clams, water and all.

Add the drained pasta to the clams and cook on low heat, stirring continuously for 1- 2 minutes in order to finish cooking the pasta in the sauce. Add more butter if needed. Garnish with parsley and serve. Enjoy...

Sammy

On July 12th, 1979, Carmine "Lilo" Galante just finished a bowl of linguine and clam sauce on an open patio at Joe & Mary's Italian-American Restaurant in Brooklyn when gunmen came in with shotguns, pistols and automatic weapons. The assassination team was well-armed and well-prepared. Lilo had declared himself Boss of the Bonanno Crime Family, and unfortunately, that's not the way it works. Like aces and eights in poker (Dead Man's hand), this meal became a dish to die for...

FETTUCCINE ALFREDO

INGREDIENTS
1 lb. egg fettuccine pasta
2 ½ cups heavy cream
12 TBSP salted butter
2 cups grated parmesan
¼ fresh lemon
1 egg yolk
Nutmeg to taste
Salt to taste
White pepper to taste

INSTRUCTIONS
Cook the pasta in a large pot of boiling salted water until tender but still firm to the bite, stirring occasionally—about 6 minutes. Drain. In a frying pan, add half the butter and melt over low heat. Stir 2 cups of the cream to blend, stirring occasionally—about 3 minutes. Slowly stir in the cheese and the remaining butter. Add the remaining cream, two large pinches of nutmeg, a little salt and white pepper to taste. Mix the fettuccine in and squeeze the lemon on top. Add the egg yolk, mixing well as it cooks.

NOTE: This is a dish that should be eaten as soon as it is done. You do not want it to start drying up on you.

Sammy

There used to be a little restaurant close to the Ravenite Social Club on Mulberry St. Any night of the week, made guys from all five families were there eating. They were famous for their Alfredo sauce. It was a small place with a dozen or so tables, and all the Wiseguys loved it.

TORTELLINI IN CREAM SAUCE

INGREDIENTS
- 1 lb. cheese tortellini (fresh made or frozen)
- 28 oz can crushed tomato
- 2 cups heavy cream
- fresh basil leaves chopped
- Virgin olive oil
- cloves of garlic sliced
- large pinches of salt, pepper, sugar

INSTRUCTIONS
In a frying pan, coat the bottom with a thin layer of virgin olive oil and add the garlic for one minute. Next, place half of the basil in to fry with the oil & garlic. Add the can of tomatoes, salt, pepper and sugar. Bring to boil then simmer. Cook tortellini in salted boiling water. Add the heavy cream to the tomato sauce using a little at a time. Mix the tortellini in the frying pan with the remaining basil. Enjoy…

NOTE: If you want to create a pink sauce you may not want to use the full 2 cups.

Sammy

When I was young, I was involved in the Colombo Family war with the Gallo brothers. We hit the mattress which meant we were going to be living together and staying put till we could kill off the other side. Guys were always cooking and one night one of the guys (I can't remember who it was) made this dish for all of us. I just remember passing the Italian bread around the table and each guy breaking off a piece and mopping up that cream sauce. It was so good I remember it like it was yesterday…

CHICKEN PEPPERONI

INGREDIENTS

1 28 oz can crushed tomatoes
1 12 oz can of tomato sauce
5 cloves garlic
1 whole chicken cut up
1 stick of pepperoni
2 oz granulated garlic chopped
2 oz grated Romano cheese
1 TBSP blk pepper
2 TBSP salt
3 oz cup of oregano
6 oz water
2 TBSP sugar

INSTRUCTIONS

In a large pot, heat the garlic with virgin olive oil. Before garlic browns, add the pepperoni (cut into tiny cubes) cook for a few minutes and add chicken, cook for ten minutes or until lightly browned. Mix the two cans of tomatoes and water together in the same pot, then add the seasonings. Add 2 TBSP sugar, bring to boil, stirring constantly so the bottom does not burn.

After the sauce reaches a boil, lower the temperature and simmer for 90 minutes. With tongs pick all the chicken out of the sauce and into a bowl. Shred the meat and return it back to the sauce without the bones and skin. Top any type of pasta with a ladle of sauce, chicken and pepperoni. Enjoy...

Sammy

I've never had this recipe before until my friend Danny made it for me and the crew. He calls it his take on the classic chicken cacciatore. It was so good a couple of the guys said this was to die for. I reminded them to be careful of what they wish for...

MUSSELS FRA DIAVOLO

INGREDIENTS

- lbs. fresh live Mussels in shells, rinsed clean
- lbs. extra virgin olive oil
- large garlic cloves, sliced
- 4 cup fresh parsley, chopped
- TBSP crushed red pepper flakes
- (28 oz) can Italian crushed tomatoes
- TBSP sugar
- 12 oz can of tomato sauce

INSTRUCTIONS

Rinse mussels under cold running water until you remove most of the sand. Fill a large pot with cold water and allow mussels to soak for at least 15 minutes. Using your fingers, pull out any beards (the hairy particles) that are visible between the shells and discard them. Transfer mussels into a colander and set aside. Throw away any mussels that are already opened. They are NOT SAFE TO EAT.

In a large pot, add the oil and fry the garlic. Before the garlic browns, add the red pepper flakes. Cook for two minutes and add the crushed tomato, tomato sauce and parsley. Cook covered for about 40 minutes, sprinkle in black pepper and if you like it extra spicy, add 2 pinches of cayenne pepper. Add the mussels and cook for about five minutes until mussels open. Any mussels that do not open are NOT SAFE TO EAT. Serve over your favorite pasta. Enjoy…

Sammy

Sammy: On April 7th, 1972, Joseph "Crazy Joe" Gallo had just left the Copacabana nightclub after watching Don Rickles perform. He was with his wife, stepdaughter, sister and one bodyguard as they made their way to Umberto's Clam House on Mulberry Street in Little Italy. They were celebrating Crazy Joe's 43rd birthday and seemed to be having a great night. Joe was enjoying his favorite dish, mussels fra Diavolo, when two gunmen came in shooting. Joe was hit but managed to get away from his family as he stumbled outside and fell onto the sidewalk. With his bodyguard wounded, Joe lay defenseless outside the restaurant when the hit team came out and finished him off.

SICILIAN RIGATONI

INGREDIENTS

1 28 oz can crushed tomatoes
1 can flat anchovies in olive oil
2 TBSP sugar
1 TBSP granulated garlic
4 cloves garlic chopped
Olive oil
Black pepper

INSTRUCTIONS

Boil water for the rigatoni. In a frying pan, add a light layer of virgin olive oil over medium heat. Add in the chopped garlic, before the garlic browns add the whole can of anchovies, oil and all. With a wooden spoon press down on the anchovies as they cook making a paste of them. Add can of tomato, sugar granulated garlic and mix well. Cover the entire top layer of the frying pan with a thin coat of blk pepper cook on med for 5 minutes and then simmer. Once the pasta is cooked al dente add it to the frying pan. Turn off the heat, mix well and enjoy...

This simple but delicious peasant dish from the land of my parents, Sicily, is quick to cook. Its rich and tasteful sauce has had many Mafioso enjoying it over the years. I remember having a bowl of this pasta in Aniello "Mr. Oneil" Dellacroce's social club. Neil was the underboss and a very powerful man, respected and feared by all in Cosa Nostra.

LEMON BAKED BRANZINO

INGREDIENTS

3 Whole branzino fish (Italian Bass)
2 whole lemons
2 garlic cloves sliced thin
Salt, pepper, granulated garlic, lemon pepper (combine and mix together)

INSTRUCTIONS

Cover a sheet pan with tin foil. Baste the bottom with a very light coat of olive oil. Take a pinch of seasoning mix and rub it on the inside of the fish and an additional pinch for the outside of the fish. Stuff the cavity with two lemon wedges and thinly-sliced garlic. Sprinkle lemon pepper mix over the top of the fish as it rests in the pan and any remaining sliced garlic. Preheat oven to 325 degrees and cook fish until fish is opaque and flakes easily with a fork—about 25 minutes. Enjoy...

NOTE: If you cannot find Branzino in your local area, try Fulton Fish Market in the Bronx. They ship it right to your door anywhere in the country!

This fish comes from the Mediterranean Sea right along the Sicilian coast; hence the nickname Italian Bass. The mafia in Sicily controls the fishing boats all along the coast. The seafood is distributed by mafia-controlled markets. It is this fish that was originally sent with a piece of clothing as a message that this person now sleeps with the fishes...

EGGPLANT PARMESAN

INGREDIENTS

3 fresh eggplants
1 lb. whole milk ricotta cheese
4-4 oz fresh mozzarella balls, sliced thin.
NOTE: you may substitute with dried shredded mozzarella if you cannot find the fresh.
4 eggs
¼ cup Romano or parmesan cheese, grated
4 cups Italian seasoned breadcrumbs
1 cup milk
Vegetable oil

Sammy

What good Italian does not like eggplant parmesan? There was an Italian deli in my old neighborhood that used to make eggplant parm sandwiches. You talk about a great sandwich – forgetaboutit!!!

INSTRUCTIONS

Take a large roasting pan or 2 half-pans and lightly oil the bottom. In a small bowl, mix the ricotta and one egg together and season with black pepper, parsley flakes and Romano cheese. In a larger bowl, add the breadcrumbs. Take another large bowl, add the remaining 3 eggs and the milk. Season with a pinch of granulated garlic, black pepper and salt. Mix well.

Cut the eggplant into round pieces about ¼ inch thick. Leave skin on! You will need a total of about 28 pieces so keep that in mind as you cut the eggplant. NOTE: Fresh eggplant dries quickly and starts to change color so you must cut, egg wash and bread crumb the slices before you cut the second eggplant. Repeat this step with the other eggplants. Now that each slice is egg washed and breaded, it is ready for frying. Fill a large frying pan halfway up with vegetable oil. Fry the eggplant for about two minutes on each side. Remove and spread out on a paper towel to soak up the excess oil.

Layer the roasting pan with the fried breaded eggplant (Since the eggplant is round, there will be some spaces. Cut up one fried eggplant and fill in the gaps). Spread the ricotta over the eggplant coins then top with the mozzarella. Place another layer of eggplant on top of the first layer, sprinkle Romano cheese and the rest of the mozzarella on top. Cover and bake for 45 minutes at 350. Enjoy…

VEAL CHOPS LA TORO

INGREDIENTS
2 cloves garlic, chopped
4 Italian frying peppers (cut lengthwise into quarters)
4 TBSP virgin olive oil
4 ¾ inch bone-in veal chops
Salt, pepper, granulated garlic, cumin (mix two pinches of each together)
Cast iron grill pan

INSTRUCTIONS
Pre-heat oven to broil.
In the cast iron pan, sauté the peppers down with virgin olive oil and chopped garlic. Mix the dry seasonings together. Lightly oil grill pan and preheat in oven for 5 minutes. While pan is heating, pat dry veal chops using paper towels. Sprinkle both sides of chops with dry rub. Place chops on heated pan and broil 7-8 minutes per side. Remove pan after you flip the chops and top with the peppers. Immediately place back in the oven for the remaining time. Once fully cooked, remove from oven and place chops on a platter to rest for 5 mins. Enjoy…
NOTE: If you can't find veal chops in your area you can substitute pork chops.

Sammy

This dish is named after me, probably because it's such a classy dish. All your fine steak houses in New York serve some type of veal chop. This simple recipe with roasted Italian peppers is my favorite.

ROASTED CHICKEN & SAUSAGE

INGREDIENTS
1 whole chicken cut into pieces
2 lbs. Italian sausage
5 lb. bag of golden potatoes
4 bell peppers
3 yellow (or white) onions

INSTRUCTIONS
Mix a few pinches of salt, pepper, cumin, oregano powder, lemon pepper and granulated garlic together. Place it to the side. Cut peppers and onions into 1-inch square pieces. In a large roasting pan, place all the chicken pieces and Italian sausage. Cut each potato into small pieces and put in the pan along with the peppers and onions. Add the seasonings and sprinkle with virgin olive oil. Mix everything together by hand. Place into a preheated 350-degree oven and bake for about two hours. Enjoy…

This family meal is cooked all together and served right in the roasting pan. Vinny Artuso was a made guy in our family and was one of the shooters on the Paul Castellano hit. Vinny had a restaurant on Arthur Ave in the Bronx called Amici's, a very nice place. Three or four of us ate there one night and they brought out a huge platter of this recipe. Four big grown men and we could not finish this wonderful meal.

STEAK PIZZAIOLA

INGREDIENTS
2 1 lb. ribeye steaks
3 yellow (or white) onions
2 bell peppers (one green, one red), julienned
2 cups mushrooms, sliced
8 cloves garlic, chopped
1 large pinch of sugar
1 12 oz can of tomato sauce
2 tbsp granulated garlic
1 tbsp salted butter
½ oz olive oil
cast iron frying pan

INSTRUCTIONS
Preheat oven to 350 Melt the butter in the pan until it's nice and hot. Sear the steaks for a minute or so on each side until a nice crust appears. Next, place frying pan in the oven. In a separate frying pan, heat the oil and add the garlic, peppers, mushrooms and onions. Sauté until slightly brown. Add the can of tomato sauce, sugar and granulated garlic and cook on medium heat for 15 minutes. Pour the sauce over the steaks and cook an additional 4 minutes in the oven. Enjoy...

On December 16th, 1985, Paul Castellano and Thomas Billotti were gunned down on their way into Sparks Steak House in Manhattan. It is the most famous mafia hit ever. Though this recipe is not on the menu at Sparks Steak House, I know for a fact it was one of Big Paul's favorite kinds of steak. Paul owned a meatpacking company and he loved his steaks. Steak pizzaiola is definitely one of the best steaks you can get.

PAPRIKA CHICKEN THIGHS

INGREDIENTS
- 2 TBSP paprika
- 1 1/2 teaspoons salt
- 3/4 tsp black pepper
- 1/2 tsp granulated garlic
- 1/4 tsp ground oregano
- 2 lbs. skin-on and bone-in chicken thighs
- 1 medium onion, thinly sliced
- 1 14-ounce can chickpeas, drained
- 3 TBSP olive oil, divided
- 1 TBSP lemon juice
- 1/4 cup chopped fresh cilantro or parsley

INSTRUCTIONS
In a large bowl, whisk together paprika, salt, granulated garlic, pepper and oregano. Pat chicken dry and toss with spices into the bowl. Cover and refrigerate for 1-2 hours.

Preheat oven to 350 degrees. In a baking dish, gently toss onions with 1 TBSP of olive oil and line onions on the bottom of the baking dish. Set aside.

Remove chicken bowl from refrigeration and add lemon juice, chickpeas and remaining olive oil. Using tongs, gently toss everything a few times to mix thoroughly. Line chicken pieces on top of the onions in the baking dish then slowly pour the chickpeas and juices throughout the dish in between chicken pieces. Bake for 45-50 minutes until the chicken reaches 165 degrees. Sprinkle with either cilantro or parsley. Enjoy...

This is another of my friend Danny's recipes and a dish he turned me onto. One of the guys in my crew had a confirmation party for his son and Danny whipped up a batch of these chicken thighs. Everyone went nuts for them and it certainly was a big hit. (Oh, not that kind of hit).

CANNOLI

INGREDIENTS

Filling only:
- ½ cup whipping cream (heavy cream)
- 15 oz container whole milk ricotta cheese (not part-skim milk – whole milk)
- ½ cup of powdered sugar
- 2 TSP vanilla
- An equal pinch of ground cinnamon & nutmeg
- 1/3 cup mini dark chocolate chips

INSTRUCTIONS

Before you begin, you must strain the ricotta overnight. Take a fine strainer that fits on top of a bowl. Cover the strainer with a cheesecloth. Pour the ricotta onto the cheesecloth and spread it evenly. Place in the fridge overnight allowing the milk to fall into the bowl; thus leaving you with strained ricotta for your dish the next day.

In a mixing bowl, whip the heavy cream with a whisk or mixer until stiff peaks form. Add the ricotta cheese, powdered sugar, vanilla, cinnamon and nutmeg into the cream. With an electric mixer, mix on medium speed until well combined—about one minute. The next step is to squeeze the whipping cream and chocolate chips into the cannoli shells. If you do not have a pastry bag, use a plastic baggy. Cut the tip of the corner off and place the cream inside.

Chill the cream for at least two hours before filling the shells. Enjoy…

NOTE: Making cannoli shells can be a little complicated. It is easy enough to buy premade shells in most supermarkets and they work just fine.

Cannoli is probably the most well-known of the Italian desserts. One of the most iconic lines in movie history is from The Godfather when they shoot Paulie in the car and fat Clemenza tells the shooter: "Leave the gun, take the cannoli." What more can you say after that…

ZEPPOLES

INGREDIENTS

1 cup warm water (about 110 degrees) warm water

1 package active dry yeast (2 1/2 teaspoons)

1 3/4 cup all-purpose flour

1/2 teaspoon salt

Vegetable oil for frying

Powdered sugar for coating

INSTRUCTIONS

In a mixing bowl, mix the yeast and water. In a separate bowl, mix the flour and salt. Once the yeast is creamy, combine with the flour/salt mixture. Cover with saran wrap and let sit for about an hour. The dough should double in size and become very airy.

About 45 minutes into the dough resting, start the fryer and heat to 375 degrees.

Using your hand or a spoon, measure a teaspoon of dough for smaller zeppoles or a tablespoon for larger zeppoles (dough balls should be the size of a golf ball) and plop the dough into the oil. NOTE: Be careful; it's hot! Also, if you do not have a fryer, you can use a pot of hot oil.

Turn continuously so all sides of the ball cook evenly, then once golden-brown, drain on a paper towel. While hot and still oily, place dough balls into a bag filled with the powdered sugar. Give them a good shake to ensure they are thoroughly covered. Enjoy…

I can still remember all the Italian festivals and the nice warm Zeppoles they served. What a treat! I have never seen an Italian feast that did not have Zeppoles, and kids as well as grownups loving them. I remember walking through the San Gennaro feast with John Gotti and a dozen other Wiseguys. We all stopped at the Zeppoles stand and tried not to get the white sugar on our nice clothes but in the end, the Zeppoles won out as we ate with complete abandon…

www.ingramcontent.com/pod-product-compliance
Lightning Source LLC
Chambersburg PA
CBHW040757240426
43673CB00014B/371